D1208277

This Journal Belongs to:

_____

Writing and compilation by Rebecca Currington and Patricia Mitchell in association with Snapdragon Group℠.

ISBN 978-1-61626-043-9

Cover design: Kirk DouPonce, DogEared Design

Published by Barbour Publishing, Inc., P.O. Box 719, Uhrichsville, Ohio 44683, www.barbourbooks.com.

Our mission is to publish and distribute inspirational products offering exceptional value and biblical encouragement to the masses.

Member of the
Evangelical Christian
Publishers Association

Printed in China.

EVERYDAY

Comfort

Journal

Rebecca Currington &
Patricia Mitchell

BARBOUR
PUBLISHING

Adversity

Adversity, calamity, hardship, misfortune, trouble, hard times—no matter what you call them, these painful episodes are part and parcel of the human experience. But you can choose not to let them bring you down, fill you with fear, and steal your attention from the blessings God has placed in your life. Look adversity square in the eye and know that your God—the God of all comfort—has an answer.

A friend loves at all times,
and a brother is born for adversity.

PROVERBS 17:17 NKJV

When you give your heart and life to God, the Bible says Jesus Christ becomes your friend and your brother—and that changes everything. You aren't alone when adversity strikes. You've become a member of God's family and part of His circle of friends. His resources are marshaled in your defense, and His loving Holy Spirit—the Bible calls Him the Comforter—is with you constantly.

Affliction

The righteous person faces many troubles,
but the LORD comes to the rescue each time.

PSALM 34:19 NLT

An affliction is any source of constant suffering in your life. That might be poverty or sickness or anxiety—only you know what you are facing. You may think that no one understands. But God does. No matter where you are, He's right there with you. Trust Him, and He will show you the way out, the way around, or the way through, and He will never leave your side.

....

....

....

....

....

....

....

....

....

Our light affliction, which is but for a moment, worketh
for us a far more exceeding and eternal weight of glory.

2 CORINTHIANS 4:17 KJV

*H*ave you ever wondered why God doesn't just put an end to your
troubles and give you a free pass from pain and suffering? After all,
He can do anything! God doesn't bring suffering to your life, but
sometimes He will ask you to walk through it for reasons known only to
Him. But you can be sure of this—God will use your affliction to make
you stronger and more secure in your faith.

Agreement

All of you should be in agreement, understanding each other,
loving each other as family, being kind and humble.

1 PETER 3:8 NCV

*G*od knows that much of our strength and comfort comes from other people—our friends and loved ones. But what if there is no one in your life who can encourage and lift you, no one who can understand what you are going through, no one who can pray with you? Don't lose heart. Set yourself in agreement with God and His will for your life. As you agree with God, He will send others to agree with you.

> This is the confidence (the assurance, the privilege of boldness) which we have in Him: [we are sure] that if we ask anything (make any request) according to His will (in agreement with His own plan), He listens to and hears us.
>
> 1 JOHN 5:14 AMP

What could be better than to be in full agreement with the One who knows the beginning from the end, someone who understands all the options and sees all the solutions? Take comfort in the fact that your prayer partner, your friend, and your comrade is God Himself. You can take any request to Him with the assurance that He will hear you. As you do, be sure to thank Him for His help.

Anxiety

Cast all your anxiety on him because he cares for you.

1 PETER 5:7

This world gives us plenty of reasons to worry. Danger looms around every corner even for the wise and well-informed. People try all kinds of things to escape worry and anxiety—recreation, yoga, video games, sleep, to name just a few. But in the end there is only one sure remedy. God says to cast all your anxiety on Him. He's big enough to handle anything that comes your way.

....

....

....

....

....

....

....

....

....

....

Do not be anxious about anything, but in
everything, by prayer and petition, with thanksgiving,
present your requests to God. And the peace of God,
which transcends all understanding, will guard
your hearts and your minds in Christ Jesus.

PHILIPPIANS 4:6–7

*W*hat does it mean to "cast your care on God"? Start by opening
your heart and telling Him about your fears, your worries, those things
that make you feel anxious. Once you've done that, thank Him for taking
all that worry off your hands. As you give up your anxious thoughts to
Him, He gives you something back—His perfect peace.

Aspirations

*I do not mean that I am already as God wants me to be.
I have not yet reached that goal, but I continue trying to
reach it and to make it mine.*

PHILIPPIANS 3:12 NCV

Are you driven by that little voice inside you that keeps telling you to reach higher, try harder, and never give up until you attain a certain goal in your life? If your goal is within the scope of God's will, that voice is almost certainly His. It isn't His will for you to seek out temporal things like money, fame, or possessions. But He does want you to aspire to become everything He has created you to be.

....

....

....

....

....

....

....

....

....

....

What matters most to me is to finish what God started.

ACTS 20:24 MSG

Who God wants you to be includes what He wants you to do. He has a specific plan for every single person in this world—including you. You may not have a grand talent or an extraordinary intellect, but you have been given everything you need to carry out your mission in life—your calling. Pray each day that God will help you find and complete the work He has given you to do.

Assurance

Faith is the assurance of things hoped for.

HEBREWS 11:1 NASB

$\mathcal{W}$e human beings have plenty of insecurities, so you shouldn't be ashamed to admit you have a few. The good news is that you don't have to let them shape your life. When you place your faith in God, they will be replaced by the steadfast assurance that those things you hope for are yours through His love and grace. No more wondering if you're good enough or lovable enough or smart enough. In God's eyes you are perfect.

> My flesh and my heart may fail, but God is the
> strength of my heart and my portion forever.
>
> PSALM 73:26

God has everything under control. That's not just a pie-in-the-sky concept—it's a fact. God knows and understands you from the inside out. And when you place your life in His hands, you can be certain that in the good times and the bad times, the happy times and the heartbreaking times, you will always have someone to depend on, someone to fall back on, someone stronger than any challenge you could possibly face.

Battles

O Sovereign LORD, my strong deliverer,
who shields my head in the day of battle. . .
PSALM 140:7

*Y*ou may be facing a battle right now—a fight for your health, your children, your finances, for example. As the battle rages, know that you are not facing the enemy alone. Your God is fighting by your side. He is leading the charge to bring you safely through. Put your confidence in Him. Follow His lead, and let His unmatched strength be a comfort to you.

_____

_____

_____

_____

_____

_____

_____

_____

_____

_____

It is God who arms me with strength and makes my way
perfect. He makes my feet like the feet of a deer; he enables
me to stand on the heights. He trains my hands for battle;
my arms can bend a bow of bronze.

PSALM 18:32–34

It could be that you have been battling for so long that you are feeling weak, exhausted, and ready to throw in the towel. Close your eyes and rest your troubled mind. Don't worry; even when you're resting, God and His army are still fighting on your behalf. And they won't stop until the battle is won. It's all right to take a break and let Him carry you for a while.

Beauty

Don't be concerned about the outward beauty of fancy hairstyles, expensive jewelry, or beautiful clothes. You should clothe yourselves instead with the beauty that comes from within, the unfading beauty of a gentle and quiet spirit, which is so precious to God.

1 PETER 3:3–4 NLT

Twenty-first-century women are exposed to an almost impossible standard of beauty. And the message is unrelenting. In such an environment, every little flaw or blemish can be devastating. God says that outward beauty is of no consequence unless there is beauty on the inside. After all, even the most beautiful woman cannot hope to keep her looks for long. The beautiful, godly soul, however, lives forever.

....

....

....

....

....

....

....

....

....

....

"The LORD does not look at the things man looks at.
Man looks at the outward appearance,
but the LORD looks at the heart."

1 SAMUEL 16:7

$\mathcal{W}$ho says what is beautiful and what is not? It would seem that the creator of a work of art would be the one whose opinion matters most. For the creator, every nuance, every brushstroke, every indention in the clay has meaning. God created you—with intention and purpose. You are His work of art. In His eyes, you are beautiful in every way, inside and out.

Belief

The older we are the more we understand the futility of this life. But there is great comfort in knowing that this life is not the end. Through His Son, Jesus Christ, God has provided a remedy for sin, with its constant menu of corruption and death. No longer are we headed only for the grave—but to the grave and beyond. This sacred belief is our blessed hope.

Jesus said to her, "I am the resurrection and the life. He who believes in me will live, even though he dies; and whoever lives and believes in me will never die. Do you believe this?"

JOHN 11:25–26

*Y*our beliefs say a lot about your future. For example, believing that hard work leads to success will help you meet your goals. Believing that true love lasts forever will help you remain steadfast in your marriage. And believing that God has promised you life everlasting will allow you to continue to value yourself even as your body ages and your earthly life winds down. Beliefs are important, and those invested in God pay the biggest dividends of all.

Belonging

We all want to belong. It's a normal human instinct. Unfortunately, our culture places value on so many things that have no lasting meaning—where we live, how we dress, where our children go to school. Comfort yourself with the truth that God values you for who you really are deep inside, nothing more, nothing less. You are His magnificent creation and a member of His royal family. You belong to Him.

_____

_____

_____

_____

_____

_____

_____

_____

_____

_____

Whether we live or die, we belong to the Lord.

ROMANS 14:8

Have you ever been abandoned by a friend or family member?
There are few feelings worse than a lost relationship. That's why it's
so important to know that once you belong to the Lord, you will always
belong to Him. Even when you mess up and make poor choices, your
heavenly Father will not abandon you. For the remainder of this life and
the life to come—you are His!

Bereavement

[Jesus said,] "Blessed are those who mourn,
for they will be comforted."

MATTHEW 5:4

*L*osing someone you love is one of the most devastating experiences in life—whether it be a friend or relative, your child or your spouse, even a beloved pet who has brightened your life and helped ward off loneliness. God understands your grief. He gave up His own precious Son for you. He knows the anguish of losing someone who meant everything to Him. Let Him comfort you as only He can.

....

....

....

....

....

....

....

....

....

....

He will swallow up death forever. The Sovereign
LORD will wipe away the tears from all faces.

ISAIAH 25:8

When you lose someone you love, you might wonder what possible
comfort anyone could give you—even God. But there is comfort in
looking beyond the grave, beyond this life, and knowing that your
separation from that beloved one, while excruciating, is not permanent.
The two of you will meet again in a place where death no longer has
meaning. Even in the darkest moments, God lights your way with hope.

Betrayal

He will shelter you with his wings. His faithful
promises are your armor and protection.

PSALM 91:4 NLT

*B*etrayal is such a bitter word. It's always personal. You invested
yourself in someone and that person purposefully turned away.
Whenever you place your trust in a human being, you risk betrayal. We
just don't have the wherewithal to remain 100 percent faithful. But God
does. And He promises never to betray the trust you place in Him. He'll
even be there to pick up the pieces, to comfort you, when others fail you.

....

....

....

....

....

....

....

....

....

"I'll marry you for good—forever! I'll marry you true
and proper, in love and tenderness. Yes, I'll marry you
and neither leave you nor let you go. You'll know me,
God, for who I really am."

HOSEA 2:19–20 MSG

*N*o other betrayal is quite as painful as the loss of marital love and
fidelity. All those bright promises of happily ever after lie broken in the
dust. If you're feeling this closest of all betrayals, God wants to comfort
you with His proposal. He wants to serve as your spiritual husband,
providing you with the love, faithfulness, compassion, guidance,
understanding, and caring you so desperately need. He won't fail you.

Boldness

[Jesus has] been through weakness and testing, experienced
it all—all but the sin. So let's walk right up to him and get
what he is so ready to give. Take the mercy, accept the help.

HEBREWS 4:15–16 MSG

God is big and powerful and holy. Even the most impressive woman
pales in His shadow. Good sense would dictate that we keep our
distance, interacting only when we are out of options. But in this case,
good sense takes a backseat to God's ways. He has invited us to be bold
with our requests, comfortable in His presence. He has called us His
children. What a wonderful privilege!

....

....

....

....

....

....

....

....

....

....

In Christ we can come before God with freedom and without fear. We can do this through faith in Christ.

EPHESIANS 3:12 NCV

*O*ur boldness before God resides in His authority, not in our own. He has set the stage for our adoption as His children, heirs to blessing and eternal life. Our part is simply to accept, to say "yes" and take our places around His table. Through faith in His love and grace, we gain bold access to His presence. Once you place your faith in who He is, you will know who you are.

Broken Heart

The LORD is close to the brokenhearted and saves those
who are crushed in spirit.

PSALM 34:18

God's love is manifest at all times in our lives, but never so much
as when our hearts are breaking. It is then that we experience His
compassion and comfort in ways we cannot even imagine during the
good times. When you've suffered a betrayal or loss or disappointment,
when life threatens to bury you under the cold, hard ground, God is
there with hope and comfort in your darkest hour.

[God] heals the brokenhearted and binds up their wounds.

PSALM 147:3

God has promised to see you through the most painful hours of your life, but His love and compassion don't end there. If you let Him, He will pick up the pieces of your broken heart and put them back together again. Your tears are precious to your heavenly Father, your suffering never wasted. You can trust Him to understand your sorrow—even enter into it with you—as He brings healing and new life from the ashes.

Burdens

Praise be to the Lord, to God our Savior,
who daily bears our burdens.

PSALM 68:19

Women are burden-carriers of the first order. In addition to our own responsibilities and troubles, we often take on those of others. God says, "You can't carry all that by yourself. Let Me help." Then He comes up alongside and helps us shoulder the load. If you feel you are faltering beneath your burdens, tell Him you are ready to let Him lend a hand. He won't touch your stuff unless you ask Him. But when you do, He'll step right up.

"Come to me, all of you who are weary and carry heavy burdens, and I will give you rest."

MATTHEW 11:28 NLT

God isn't going to snap His fingers and make your financial woes disappear. You will still have to deal with your problem children and bear responsibility for your aging parents or your boss's unrealistic expectations. But God will faithfully provide solutions, like help from other human hands, wisdom, and counsel. And He'll give you a place of rest along the way—like a well-watered oasis in the desert.

Challenges

Just as the sufferings of Christ flow over into our lives,
so also through Christ our comfort overflows.

2 CORINTHIANS 1:5

*A*re you facing an extreme challenge in your life—perhaps your
children are rebelling, your marriage is floundering, your health is
in peril, your finances are out of control? Jesus had challenges as
well—big ones. He was subjected to all manner of indignities, pain, and
suffering. Although He submitted Himself to those cruel circumstances
for our sake, in God's perfect time He rose up and conquered both sin
and death.

_____

_____

_____

_____

_____

_____

_____

_____

_____

_____

Because the Sovereign LORD helps me, I will not be
disgraced. Therefore have I set my face like flint,
and I know I will not be put to shame.

ISAIAH 50:7

*E*ven though God uses certain negative situations in our lives to
strengthen and equip us, He doesn't cause our adverse circumstances.
Most often they are the result of our own poor choices or the poor
choices of others. Ask God to accomplish His will in your life and then
help you rise up and conquer your challenges—just as Jesus did.

Children

This is what the LORD says. . . "I will comfort you
as a mother comforts her child."

ISAIAH 66:12–13 NCV

*R*aising children is the most difficult, rewarding, exhausting,
beautiful, chaotic, amazing job a woman can have. It's a mixed bag of
dynamic emotions, pure affections, and unwavering devotion. When
her children need comfort, a true mother instinctively provides it. God
is the same way with His children. When you are hurting, He is there
without fail, reaching out to you.

_____

_____

_____

_____

_____

_____

_____

_____

_____

He gives childless couples a family,
gives them joy as the parents of children.

PSALM 113:9 MSG

*S*ome women live with a strong, unrelenting longing for children that seems to go unanswered. If you are dealing with this heartache, you can know that God has placed the desire to be a mother in your heart—and not just to frustrate you. Perhaps it's time to consider other possibilities. We are ourselves adopted into His family, and someone must mother those young in the faith. Ask God to help you find the children He has ordained for you.

Confidence

In the fear of the LORD there is strong confidence.
PROVERBS 14:26 NKJV

*E*verywhere we look there are messages about how to be filled with inner confidence. Take this course, dress this way, speak your mind, and the ever-popular suggestion to reach down deep inside yourself. Unfortunately, those tactics only give the illusion of confidence. True confidence comes from knowing that almighty God, the creator and sustainer of the universe, is backing you up and showing you the way.

....

....

....

....

....

....

....

....

....

....

Do not throw away your confidence;
it will be richly rewarded.

HEBREWS 10:35

*C*ircumstances of life often tend to erode our confidence and leave us feeling weak and unproductive. When you encounter those times, don't throw away your confidence—redirect it. Make sure that it is anchored in God's character, resources, and unwavering faithfulness. People will fail you, and you will even fail yourself at times, but God will never let you down.

Creativity

By him all things were created:
things in heaven and on earth, visible and invisible,
whether thrones or powers or rulers or authorities;
all things were created by him and for him.

COLOSSIANS 1:16

God is quite the Master Artist, and He takes His work seriously. You may have noticed the delicious burnt umber of the sunset, the yellow-green waters of Lake Superior, or a towering stand of timber. Yes, that was His work. The entire universe is His gallery. But those spectacular pieces are little more than eye candy compared to His human creations. God expressed His extraordinary creativity when He created you—and He calls you His best work.

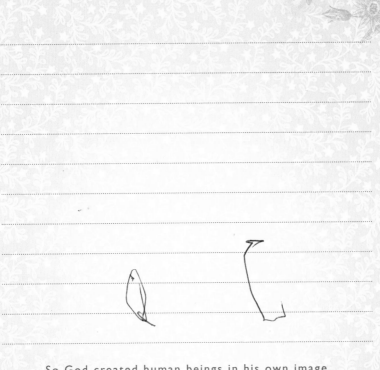

So God created human beings in his own image.
In the image of God he created them;
male and female he created them.

GENESIS 1:27 NLT

*D*id you know you were created in God's image? No wonder you feel that urge to create. Don't hold back. Open your mind to new thoughts, new mental pictures, new ways of doing things. Ask God to open wide the gates of your creativity. You may not be an artist or a musician or a writer, but God has given each person—including you—a creative bent, and He is eager for you to find yours.

Danger

"Whoever listens to me will live in safety
and be at ease, without fear of harm."

PROVERBS 1:33

*R*emember the Ten Commandments? Many people think making those rules was God's way of asserting His authority, making sure we all know He's in charge. But a closer look shows that He is more interested in keeping us safe in a dangerous world. Just as you institute guidelines to keep your children out of harm's way, our loving heavenly Father has done the same.

....

....

....

....

....

....

....

....

....

....

....

....

....

....

....

....

....

....

....

The wise see danger ahead and avoid it.

PROVERBS 27:12 NCV

It probably isn't possible to avoid all danger in this treacherous world, but living wisely and paying attention to God's Word can give you a real advantage. Parents often establish rules for their family that the kids don't understand. But parents know the rules are for the kids' safety and well-being. Sometimes you won't see the reason for God's rules either, but obeying them will help you skirt danger and abide in safety.

Debt

Let no debt remain outstanding,
except the continuing debt to love one other.

ROMANS 13:8

*I*t's rare to find anyone in our current culture who is truly debt free. Financial advisors even contend that some calculated debt is an advantage. The trouble is that debt can quickly spiral out of control. If you're facing a mountain of debt each month, you know how hopeless it feels. God wants you to be free—free to fulfill your destiny. If you ask Him, He'll help you find a plan to free yourself.

....

....

....

....

....

....

....

....

....

....

God called you to be free, but do not use your freedom
as an excuse to do what pleases your sinful self.

GALATIANS 5:13 NCV

*F*reeing yourself from debt will take some work. It may mean
sacrifices, changing your way of doing things, replacing bad habits with
good ones. But you can be sure that God will be behind you all the way.
He'll provide comfort, wisdom, and encouragement along the way. He'll
even give you favor with your creditors. And the day you wake up and
realize you are free will be worth it all.

Deception

Jesus answered, "I am the way, and the truth, and the life. The only way to the Father is through me."

JOHN 14:6 NCV

If you've ever been deceived, you know how devastating it can be. Not only do you feel hurt, but your sense of trust is shaken, as well. Maybe that's why God so often reminds us in the Bible that He represents truth, pure and simple. There is no deception in Him. He won't try to secure your love with empty promises. He can be trusted. Wrap your heart and mind around that truth and let it heal you.

_____

_____

_____

_____

_____

_____

_____

_____

_____

_____

The heart is deceitful above all things and beyond cure.
Who can understand it?

JEREMIAH 17:9

*G*od knows we are vulnerable to deception not only from others but also from our own hearts. We humans have an innate inclination to lie to ourselves. But God has a remedy. He encourages us to follow Him, listen to Him, trust His words. Can you trust your heart? The sweet Holy Spirit—the Comforter—will help you keep your heart clean and filled with truth.

Defeat

We have troubles all around us, but we are
not defeated. We do not know what to do,
but we do not give up the hope of living.

2 CORINTHIANS 4:8 NCV

Sometimes it seems like one little thing goes wrong, and it starts a chain reaction of disappointments and negative expectations. The power of this process is in its cumulative nature. Like the straw that breaks the camel's back, one defeat sits on another until it brings us down. God says His mercies are new every morning. Each day is a new beginning. He wants us to put our troubles behind us and cling to the hope of living.

....

....

....

....

....

....

....

....

....

....

With God we will gain the victory.

PSALM 108:13

God wants us to understand that even though we will experience troubles, we are immune to lasting defeat. Even when we lose, we win because God sees to it that we gain wisdom and understanding from our losses. He reaches out to us with comfort and consolation. Each loss actually brings us closer to victory. Learn from your defeats, and then turn your back on them and reach for God's mercies.

Depression

Be strong and take heart, all you who hope in the LORD.
PSALM 31:24

For those who live with the darkness of depression, no one has to explain the pain and despair. It's not the kind of thing that can be reasoned away. It's just there, pulling them down, keeping them captive. If you suffer depression, you should know that God doesn't intend for His children to live in despair. He has an answer for you. Visit your doctor for a check-up, find someone to talk to. When you do what you can, He will be there to do the rest.

Why are you downcast, O my soul?
Why so disturbed within me? Put your hope in God,
for I will yet praise him, my Savior and my God.

PSALM 42:5–6

$\mathcal{D}$epression is often a physiological problem, but just as often it's a result of adverse circumstances. If events in your life have left you in the depths of despair, God wants you to know that you are not alone. He is right there with you. Even when others don't understand, He does. Others only see who you are on the outside, but He knows all about you, inside and out. He knows how to comfort you. Reach out to Him and He will reach back.

Desires

May He grant you according to your heart's desire,
and fulfill all your purpose.

PSALM 20:4 NKJV

 What is it you want with all your heart—true love, a great job, children? Only you know what it is. You needn't hold back. Because you are His child, God longs to give you the things that would make you happy. There are some conditions, though. Like any good parent, He balances what you want with what He knows is good for you. He isn't interested in your temporary, superficial happiness. He wants to give you more than you ever imagined.

....

....

....

....

....

....

....

....

....

....

Delight yourself in the Lord and he will
give you the desires of your heart.

PSALM 37:4

As you get to know God better, as you bask in His love and care, your
desires will change. Selfishness and unwholesome desires will fade
away. You will begin to understand and desire those things He desires
for you—those things that will resonate in your heart and bring you true
happiness. God created you, and He knows you better than you know
yourself. Trust Him to give you the desires of your heart.

Determination

"Be strong and do not give up,
for your work will be rewarded."

2 CHRONICLES 15:7

*H*ave you ever watched a marathon? They can be pretty boring until the runners get to the final few miles. Some are so exhausted that they can barely stay on their feet. You want to scream, "Give it up! It's just a race!" but they don't give up. The runners are determined to finish. They understand the reward that awaits them on the other side of the finish line, so they keep pushing. That's the kind of determination it takes to please God.

_____

_____

_____

_____

_____

_____

_____

_____

_____

> Let us hold fast the confession of our hope without
> wavering, for He who promised is faithful.
>
> HEBREWS 10:23 NKJV

God doesn't want you to ever give up on becoming the person He created you to be. He wants to see you follow the dream He's placed in your heart, develop your talent, fulfill your mission in life. Sure, sometimes you will feel like giving up, trying something easier. But remember that a reward waits for you on the other side of the finish line—a reward more wonderful than you can imagine. You can count on that because God has promised.

Discipleship

Jesus said, "If you hold to my teaching,
you are really my disciples. Then you will know
the truth, and the truth will set you free."

JOHN 8:31-32

Sometimes trying to follow the teachings of Jesus makes you feel as if you're going two steps forward and one step back. The "step back" shouldn't leave you discouraged, however. Instead, let it encourage you to turn to God with a humble heart. He promises to send His Holy Spirit to fill you with strength, confidence, and perseverance as you step forward again in His footsteps.

....

....

....

....

....

....

....

....

....

....

[Jesus said,] "A new command I give you: Love one another.
As I have loved you, so you must love one another.
By this all men will know that you are my disciples,
if you love one another."

JOHN 13:34–35

*H*e's hard to love." "She's not a lovable person." Whose name
comes to mind? This is the very person Jesus invites you to love the
same way He loves you—with a heart open to forgiveness, kindness,
and compassion. As you follow in Jesus' footsteps, let the Holy Spirit
replace your feelings of dislike, anger, or resentment with a disciple's
willingness to reach out in genuine fellowship and Christian love.

Divorce

My comfort in my suffering is this:
Your promise preserves my life.

PSALM 119:50

Divorce can leave lifelong consequences in its wake, even affecting and infecting future relationships. Though you may be facing some of the negative results of divorce, God offers a positive message: He forgives you, regardless of what you may have said and done. And He comforts you with His unchanging promise of everlasting love and eternal life. Just ask Him, and He'll tell you as many times as you need to hear it.

....

....

....

....

....

....

....

....

....

Mercy triumphs over judgment!

JAMES 2:13

*D*ivorce isn't really just a struggle between two people. It usually ends up involving friends and family. It's difficult to come away without some bitter feelings toward someone. Emotions so strong make it very tough to forgive. But that's exactly what you must do before you can move on with your life. Ask God to help you let go of any bitterness you might be harboring. Then turn your face to the future and the bright tomorrows ahead.

Doubts

What if some did not have faith? Will their lack
of faith nullify God's faithfulness? Not at all!

ROMANS 3:3-4

*W*hen you doubt God's power and ability, you then place your trust in someone or something else. Sooner or later, you're sadly disappointed, because no one is capable of meeting your spiritual needs, and no thing or activity on earth can meet your deep longing for fulfillment. Only God can! Throw doubt aside and come back to Him. No matter how long you have been gone, He has been faithful to you and will be there for you.

_____

_____

_____

_____

_____

_____

_____

_____

_____

> [Jesus] said to them, "Why are you troubled,
> and why do doubts rise in your minds?"
>
> LUKE 24:38

God never condemns you for doubting. Instead, He invites you to use doubt as a springboard to find out more about Him, His love for you, and His plan for you to live with Him in heaven. Give voice to your doubts, looking to Him for answers through Bible study, meditation, and the counsel of mature Christians. Let your doubts work to take you toward a greater appreciation of your God and His unwavering love for you.

Dreams

For God is working in you, giving you the desire
and the power to do what pleases him.

PHILIPPIANS 2:13 NLT

When "no" evicts your cherished hopes and dreams, bitterness often moves in—and stays. Avoid the temptation to let disappointment replace your dreams, and instead let God's Spirit find a home in your heart. Tell Him your dreams then listen for His answer. Discover His "yes" in the blessings around you, in your abilities and opportunities, and in the work He has given you to do. Let following Him be your dream come true!

_____

_____

_____

_____

_____

_____

_____

_____

Who hopes for what he already has? But if we hope for
what we do not yet have, we wait for it patiently.

ROMANS 8:24–25

God has no desire for you to be misled by lies that masquerade as truth. While popular myths and wishful thinking sometimes offer feel-good solutions, God has given you His Word so you can know the difference between dreams and reality. He invites you to immerse yourself, not in wishful thinking that evaporates in a day, but in sound teachings that will lead you to the truth and remain with you throughout eternity.

Duty

Whatever work you do, do your best.

ECCLESIASTES 9:10 NCV

*B*y necessity, many people work in jobs they don't like or feel suited for. For them, work is a duty rather than a dream. If you find yourself in that situation, there is something you can do. Take one day at a time and focus your attention on your responsibilities for that day. Give it your all as a token of your love and respect for God. You will either begin to see your job differently, or God will find you a new assignment. He always rewards the diligent.

....

....

....

....

....

....

....

....

....

Commit to the LORD whatever you do,
and your plans will succeed.

PROVERBS 16:3

God is never without a plan, and He has one for your life as well. There will be times when you wonder how your current job could be part of that plan. Maybe you are just spinning your wheels, doing your duty. Be assured that God has a purpose for everything you put your hand to. Perhaps it's a lesson you need to learn or a skill you will one day need. Begin to look at your job in the context of God's wisdom, and you'll see His hand in all you do.

Emotion

Weeping may remain for a night,
but rejoicing comes in the morning.

PSALM 30:5

When your emotions leave you sitting at the bottom of a dark pit, it's hard to believe in daylight. That's why the Bible speaks so clearly on the fleeting nature of human feelings and the eternal nature of God's presence and His love. He sends you dawn after night, spring after winter, joy after sorrow, to remind you that even in the depths of sorrow, there is the height—and the light—of His love.

> The LORD hath heard the voice of my weeping.
> The LORD hath heard my supplication;
> the LORD will receive my prayer.
>
> PSALM 6:8–9 KJV

God has not abandoned you in your weeping. Neither does He judge you for your feelings, nor does He offer you a useless platitude in response to your sorrow. Instead, He comforts you by opening His arms to you, inviting you to talk to Him about your feelings and the depth of your emotions. Even more, He promises He will listen. Go to Him in confidence, even if you're not sure what to say. He is listening to you.

Emptiness

It was not with perishable things such as silver or gold that you were redeemed from the empty way of life handed down to you from your forefathers, but with the precious blood of Christ, a lamb without blemish or defect.

1 PETER 1:18–19

A deep feeling of emptiness drives many to addiction, despair, and risky behavior. Without a sense of meaning and purpose in their lives, who could blame them? Maybe you find yourself in that very place—empty through and through—but you don't have to live that way. God loves you and He has a purpose and plan for your life—a plan that will challenge you and bring you joy and fulfillment. Let Him fill you with His Holy Spirit and show you who you were created to be.

....

....

....

....

....

....

....

....

....

I pray that you, being rooted and established in love, may
have power, together with all the saints, to grasp how wide
and long and high and deep is the love of Christ, and to
know this love that surpasses knowledge—that you may be
filled to the measure of all the fullness of God.

EPHESIANS 3:17–19

Empty calories lurk in foods of no nutritional value. Similarly, empty
emotions are hidden in foolish thoughts, selfish pursuits, and meaningless
activities. They leave you unfulfilled, never satisfying your real needs. God's
love isn't like that—it's deep, refreshing, renewing, restoring, and loaded
with spiritual nutrients. Breathe it in! Swallow it! Fill yourself with it! You will
never feel empty again.

Endurance

Let us run with endurance the race that is set before us,
looking unto Jesus, the author and finisher of our faith.

HEBREWS 12:1–2 NKJV

*Y*ou long to scream "enough!" and turn your back on everything, but
you don't. At times like this, God raises your spiritual eyes to Jesus, the
one who not only walks with you but has gone before you to the end.
Trust Him to take you to the finish. There you will thank Him for making
it possible for you to endure present hardship and reap the eternal
reward of achieving His purpose for your life.

_____

_____

_____

_____

_____

_____

_____

_____

_____

When your endurance is fully developed, you will be
perfect and complete, needing nothing.

JAMES 1:4 NLT

How easy it would be to give up! And the truth is, many people would.
Yet deep in your heart you know God asks you to carry on until you
receive God-given release. Why? Because He has full spiritual maturity
in mind for you. You may be unable to figure out how your current
situation can lead you to a fuller, more joyful tomorrow, but God knows.
Put your trust in Him as you continue on the way He has laid out for you.

Envy

Love is patient, love is kind. It does not envy,
it does not boast, it is not proud.

1 CORINTHIANS 13:4

*W*hen envy fills the heart, there's no room left for love. If you have been sidetracked by envy, ask God to help you regain your thoughts and emotions by forgiving you and putting you back on the right path. Once the Lord sweeps your heart clean, you will have a dwelling place fit for humility, kindliness, compassion, and love.

Don't for a minute envy careless rebels; soak yourself
in the Fear-of-God—That's where your future lies.
Then you won't be left with an armload of nothing.

PROVERBS 23:17 MSG

*Y*ou see people living in carefree disregard of God's "thou shalt nots."
When they appear so lighthearted and happy, it's hard not to envy them.
But you should not. Their lives are headed nowhere. Turn your admiring
glance instead to God's Word and read His promises for those who walk
rightly. There is great comfort in knowing that following Him will bring
you a lifetime—and eternity—of joy.

Eternal Life

[Jesus said,] "I tell you the truth, whoever hears my word and believes him who sent me has eternal life and will not be condemned; he has crossed over from death to life."

JOHN 5:24

When you're tempted to live for the moment, consider this: God has given you eternal life right now. God means for you to give up a human, shortsighted perspective and live as if you're living for eternity—because you are. Ask God to allow His Spirit to stretch your spiritual sight beyond this moment. Let Him show you what matters for all eternity; then commit yourself to live in it.

....

....

....

....

....

....

....

....

....

[Jesus said,] "God so loved the world that he gave
his one and only Son, that whoever believes in
him shall not perish but have eternal life."

JOHN 3:16

*W*hy would almighty God love me?" you ask. "And why would He open heaven to me when I've done nothing to deserve it?" Yes, God's unconditional love is beyond human understanding, but it's there for you. His plan of salvation is all about taking who you are and making you who you were created to be. No matter how strongly you may feel you don't deserve God, embrace Him as firmly and as tenderly as He embraces you.

Example

To this you were called, because Christ suffered for you,
leaving you an example, that you should follow in his steps.

1 PETER 2:21

*E*ven Jesus' closest disciples—men and women who traveled
with Him during His earthly ministry—did not always follow His
example. At times they bickered among themselves, doubted His
words, misunderstood His ministry, and denied they even knew Him.
Nonetheless, Jesus' healing forgiveness was there for them, just as it is
for you. Ask Him and He will teach you how to walk in His footsteps.

....

....

....

....

....

....

....

....

....

Be an example to the believers in word,
in conduct, in love, in spirit, in faith, in purity.

1 TIMOTHY 4:12 NKJV

*W*hen you consider how many people you influence every day through your words, attitude, and actions, you realize how often you set a less-than-stellar example. God uses these times to impress on you how much He wants you to make Him a vital part of your life—not just when it's easy but every day, every hour, every minute. Let your entire life become an example of His love for you.

Expectation

In the morning, O LORD, you hear my voice; in the morning
I lay my requests before you and wait in expectation.

PSALM 5:3

*Y*ou have taken your heartfelt requests to God, and now you are waiting
for His response. Don't grow impatient. Instead, relish this time of
hopeful expectation. Rehearse the ways God has come through for you
in the past. Allow thanksgiving to flow freely from your lips. Like a child
on the day before her birthday, enjoy a confident excitement concerning
what God is going to do on your behalf. He is a gracious Father who can be
trusted without hesitation.

My soul, wait silently for God alone,
for my expectation is from Him.

PSALM 62:5 NKJV

Sometimes people fail to live up to your expectations, and sometimes you fail to live up to the values and standards you have for yourself. As you take your hurt, your embarrassment, your shame to God, don't forget His unchangeable love for you. He has promised you the gift of His Holy Spirit to give you strength and comfort, and you should expect no less. He will never fail you.

Experience

We know that in all things God works for the
good of those who love him, who have
been called according to his purpose.

ROMANS 8:28

Perhaps God is permitting you to undergo an unhappy or hurtful
experience, and you understandably wonder why. How can He stand by
and let you suffer? While the reason why may remain unanswered this
side of heaven, His care for you and involvement in your life is a given. He
will use this experience to draw you closer to Him, and in it He will bring
about good.

....

....

....

....

....

....

....

....

....

....

You will show me the way of life, granting me the joy of
your presence and the pleasures of living with you forever.

PSALM 16:11 NLT

How long has it been since you allowed yourself to experience the
spiritual joys of life? Don't let the day's troubles, a busy schedule, and
other distractions strip you of the everyday pleasures God has set before
you. Consider the fact He has called you to be His own. Meditate on His
presence in your life and what it means to you. Give thanks today for the
blessings of the day, and experience His love for you!

Failure

If we are unfaithful, he remains faithful,
for he cannot deny who he is.

2 TIMOTHY 2:13 NLT

*Y*ou have fallen down, and now what? God is waiting to pick you up again, to dust you off, to comfort and strengthen you so you can go on. Even if you've fallen because you strayed from God's commandments, His strong arms still wait for you. All you need do is call out to Him and ask Him to help you get back on your feet again. God is waiting. Reach up to Him!

Everyone born of God overcomes the world. This is the
victory that has overcome the world, even our faith.

1 JOHN 5:4

*Y*ou are living your faith, but to some people you're a failure. You fail
to measure success by the world's standards, and you fail to go along
with popular thinking and adopt ungodly values as your own. Let your
soul be glad when people call you a failure, because it proves your faith
is evident to others. In God's eyes, you have conquered the world. You
have rich fellowship with Him and a future brighter than the sun.

Family Life

Bear with each other and forgive whatever grievances you
may have against one another. Forgive as the Lord forgave
you. And over all these virtues put on love, which binds them
all together in perfect unity.

COLOSSIANS 3:13–14

*N*o family is perfect, and nearly everyone will at some time hurt, betray, and disappoint a family member. In extreme cases it may be necessary to distance yourself. But in all cases, it is necessary to forgive. Let God judge the person or people who caused the pain. To you He says, "Forgive." When you do, you will no longer harm yourself with the corrosive emotions of anger and resentment. Instead, you will become more like Christ, who long ago forgave you.

....

....

....

....

....

....

....

....

....

....

Live in harmony with one another.

ROMANS 12:16

*W*hy all the arguments, the bitterness, the ugly words? In your home, everyone feels tense and defensive, and you know this is not what God intends for your family. Let Him put things right, beginning with you. Ask His Spirit to show you how to live in godly harmony with all the members of your family. Let Him teach you the words and actions that create genuine affection and lasting unity. Let God's peace begin with you and comfort everyone with His presence.

Faults

Confess your faults one to another, and pray one
for another, that ye may be healed.

JAMES 5:16 KJV

*C*riticism hurts. While your first reaction is, quite naturally, to retaliate, God has an alternative in mind. Listen to the words of your critic, He says. If your critic has pinpointed a fault in your conduct or character, give thanks you have someone in your life who is frank and truthful enough to tell you where you need to make changes. Ask the Holy Spirit to help you mature and grow in this area.

_____

_____

_____

_____

_____

_____

_____

_____

_____

All Scripture is inspired by God and is useful for teaching,
for showing people what is wrong in their lives, for
correcting faults, and for teaching how to live right.

2 TIMOTHY 3:16 NCV

*I*f you feel uncomfortable when you read God's commandments and
hear His guidelines for your life, good! The discomfort you feel when
facing your faults means the Holy Spirit is at work in you, molding you
more and more into a living, breathing, active, vibrant follower of Jesus
Christ. Welcome your discomfort. Pray about the faults God's Word
points out, and learn what you need to do to overcome them.

Fear

I will fear no evil, for you are with me;
your rod and your staff, they comfort me.

PSALM 23:4

Do you find yourself trembling when television newscasters predict hard times ahead? Could things really get as bad as they say? Take heart! God reaches out to you, as He has to His people throughout history, and offers His comfort in a world full of uncomfortable news and troublesome events. No matter what happens or doesn't happen, your all-powerful and all-knowing God is your strength and salvation. You can rest at ease in Him.

> "Fear not, for I have redeemed you;
> I have summoned you by name; you are mine."
>
> ISAIAH 43:1

In a world of more than six billion souls, fear of becoming "just a number" ranks high among modern-day stressors. God removes the reason for your nagging fear of anonymity when He says to you, "I know your name" and "You are mine." He loves you personally, and He claims you personally. In Jesus Christ, you possess an eternal identity as a forgiven and beloved child of God.

Forgiveness

You are a forgiving God, gracious and compassionate,
slow to anger and abounding in love.

NEHEMIAH 9:17

Perhaps the sin was huge, and you're still suffering its consequences. Even though you feel deeply sorry for what you did and have apologized to those you hurt, guilt burdens your heart and weighs your spirit. Do not let that sin continue on its damaging rampage through your soul. Instead, give your sorrow to the God who is bigger than any sin you could possibly commit. Be comforted by His promise of restoration and renewal, and go forward in forgiveness.

Make allowance for each other's faults, and forgive
anyone who offends you. Remember, the Lord
forgave you, so you must forgive others.

COLOSSIANS 3:13 NLT

No one wants to be the first to say "I'm sorry." No one jumps to
take responsibility for a misspoken word, a hurtful act, a mismanaged
situation. But without someone possessing the humble courage to
extend the hand of peace, no healing can ever take place. Do your part
by stepping forward, admitting your part, and asking forgiveness of
anyone you may have offended. Jesus forgave you first. True heart
healing begins with your willingness to be first in the same way.

Freedom

The LORD sets prisoners free.
PSALM 146:7

We take for granted the ability to move about at will, make independent choices, and manage our own affairs. Many in this world are not so fortunate. They are prisoners. Some are being held in prison for illegal acts; others live in nations where they are prisoners by the will of the government. Still others are prisoners of their own behaviors and excesses. To all the prisoners, God offers the freedom to receive His love and grace, the freedom to know Him and serve Him. Are you in need of freedom?

_____

_____

_____

_____

_____

_____

_____

_____

_____

_____

Where the Spirit of the Lord is, there is freedom.

2 CORINTHIANS 3:17 NCV

Though some might think of the Christian way as paved with restrictions, just the opposite is true. In the Christian message, God offers you the priceless freedom of living each day free from the chains of guilt, despair, and hopelessness. He has opened to you the door to freedom as His Spirit directs you along the path He has laid out for you—a path leading to genuine happiness and lasting liberty.

Friendship

Wounds from a friend can be trusted.

PROVERBS 27:6

It could be that a friend told you the truth, and it hit you hard. Resentment welled up inside you, and you had to bite your tongue not to say anything. Now you wonder if your friendship will ever be the same again. No, it won't be. It will be better. In her, you have a friend who thinks enough of you to share her deepest concerns, no matter how sensitive or difficult the subject. Give thanks to God for the comfort of a true friend.

As iron sharpens iron, so a friend sharpens a friend.

PROVERBS 27:17 NLT

*T*he angry words really flew between the two of you, and now you wonder if there's anything left of your friendship. When friendship proves challenging, consider how God can use the situation. He may have something to show the two of you about learning from and growing with each other. He may be pushing both of you toward a deeper, more fulfilling friendship—a friendship meant to last a lifetime.

Fulfillment

A longing fulfilled is a tree of life.

PROVERBS 13:12

*Y*our deepest longings and cherished dreams hold a special place in your heart, and they hold a special place in God's heart, too. He cares what you care about. If you yearn for the fulfillment of your dreams and desires, bring them to the One who knows all about needs, desires, longings, yearnings—and miracles. Trust Him to draw from your dreams the pleasure of godly fulfillment and the satisfaction of true contentment.

_____

_____

_____

_____

_____

_____

_____

_____

_____

_____

I cry out to God Most High, to God,
who fulfills {his purpose} for me.

PSALM 57:2

*Y*ou have looked for fulfillment in many places but have discovered
nothing but worthless promises. You are not alone! Throughout the
Bible, people just like you have raised empty hands to God, begging Him
to soothe the deepest longing of their hearts. He heard their pleas, and
He hears yours, too. Look to Him. Let His Holy Spirit show you how to
find true and lasting fulfillment in living as the beloved child He has
created you to be.

Giving

Give freely and spontaneously. Don't have a stingy heart.
The way you handle matters like this triggers GOD, your God's,
blessing in everything you do, all your work and ventures.

DEUTERONOMY 15:10 MSG

*F*und-raisers and donation campaigns ignite guilt feelings. We begrudgingly pledge a small amount, then we add to our guilt the feeling of being manipulated into giving. God wants a whole new attitude. He stands ready to bless the generous giver, the one who gives with a genuinely cheerful heart. Remember, you possess nothing now that God hasn't given you in the first place. Let your giving flow from a heart of gratitude and love.

....

....

....

....

....

....

....

....

....

....

> [Jesus said,] "Give, and it will be given to you. A good measure, pressed down, shaken together and running over, will be poured into your lap. For with the measure you use, it will be measured to you."
>
> LUKE 6:38

*I*f you want more, give more. That's God's way, and He invites you to make it your way, too. He promises you abundance when you generously share your time, efforts, resources, and abilities. Do so without expecting a reward, knowing all along God will reward you in far greater measure than you can imagine, in far more directions than you expect. Give His way a try, and find out for yourself.

Grace

How rich is God's grace, which he
has given to us so fully and freely.

EPHESIANS 1:7–8 NCV

You may be having a difficult time accepting God's undeserved love.
Instead, you expect to pay for what you buy and work for what you earn.
When it comes to His undeserved love—His grace—you bring the
same thinking with you. God's grace, however, works differently. His
grace is yours, and it isn't possible to pay for it, earn it, or deserve it.
God's grace is yours, not because of you, but because of God.

....

....

....

....

....

....

....

....

....

....

From the fullness of his grace we have
all received one blessing after another.

JOHN 1:16

Have you ever shown kindness to someone "just because"? God
works in a similar way. He is kind, gracious, and generous toward you
"just because." His "just because" relieves you of the burden of striving
for His affection and worrying He will fall out of love with you. Today,
relax in His grace—His all-embracing love for you. Open your arms,
and accept His love.

Gratitude

Give thanks to the LORD, for he
is good; his love endures forever.

PSALM 107:1

*D*o you regularly count your blessings—the beauty and variety of wildflowers, the immensity of the evening sky, the power of the ocean's waves, the majestic heights of a mountain? Even when you forget to say thank you, God surrounds you with these things every day. Name three things in creation you take pleasure in and give thanks to God for each of them. Your God made them for you simply because He wanted you to enjoy them.

_____

_____

_____

_____

_____

_____

_____

_____

_____

Thank God no matter what happens.

I THESSALONIANS 5:18 MSG

*I*f you are going through a difficult time in your life, your prayers may sound more like a list of woes than a song of thanksgiving. God wants you to bring to Him your cries of pain, but He also invites you to offer Him your thanks for the good things happening in your life. This is how He reminds you that you and the situation you're facing remain in His hands. Be thankful, because God is present with you—loving and comforting you—every moment of every day.

Honesty

Good people will be guided by honesty.

PROVERBS 11:3 NCV

*H*ave you ever been tempted to try a little sleight-of-hand—some deception that will give you an edge over someone else or a privilege you want? Even if we pride ourselves on being clever, God calls it something else: dishonest. For all who strive to follow Him, God sets clear directions to guide thought, speech, conduct, and relationships. With the help of the Holy Spirit, commit yourself to honesty in all you say and do.

Light shines on those who do right;
joy belongs to those who are honest.

PSALM 97:11 NCV

When you're honest and forthright in all things, you never need worry about covering your tracks or being exposed. You can live with a lightness of spirit unknown to those who must glance over their shoulders in fear of being found out. Ask God to show you where you need to act in a more upright and blameless way. With the help of His Spirit working in you, resolve that your relationships and dealings will be marked by godly honesty.

Hope

We who have fled to take hold of the hope offered to us
may be greatly encouraged. We have this hope as an anchor
for the soul, firm and secure.

HEBREWS 6:18–19

*W*ithout hope, you may feel as if you're being swept along by chaotic currents, unable to grasp anything solid. God wants you to know that He is about to reach you, lift you up, and set your feet on the firm ground of His Word and His promises. Though He might not reveal to you the reasons behind current circumstances, He invites you to place your hope in Him, holding firmly and securely to the certainty of His love and care for you.

No one whose hope is in you will ever be put to shame.

PSALM 25:3

God has given us His promises in order to provide sure footing in a tumultuous world. He knew we wouldn't be helped by promises filled with ambiguity and double-talk, so He gives it to us straight. Put your hope in Me, He says, and you won't be disappointed. No one will call you a fool—not after they see your God working on your behalf. Placing your hope in Him is a no-risk proposition, because He will never fail you.

Humility

With humility comes wisdom.

PROVERBS 11:2 NLT

In a misguided desire to appear humble, some people intentionally downplay their abilities and achievements. Your abilities and achievements, however, are unique gifts your God has given to you. Godly humility would have you accept them with pure gratitude and do your best to use them to their fullest. When someone praises you, thank your thoughtful friend then add, "To God be the glory!" This is heavenly humility—and the height of wisdom.

....

....

....

....

....

....

....

....

....

Humility and the fear of the Lord
bring wealth and honor and life.

PROVERBS 22:4

Though no one seems eager to pick up a person fallen from the pedestal of pride, God is willing. If you find you have to pick yourself up after a humiliating feat of your own making, know this: God still loves you. He desires to hold you close and help you learn from your experience. Even at your lowest point, you are precious to Him. Give Him your hand and He will help you find your footing again.

Illness

"I am the LORD who heals you."

EXODUS 15:26 NKJV

*H*ave you thought of your illness as a mirror for God's power? When you remain faithful to Him despite your weakness, refusing to give in to despair, people notice. They wonder, "Where does she get her courage?" "How can he remain so optimistic?" Ask the Holy Spirit to reveal His presence in you and use your weakness to reflect His strength. In your illness, people will see the power of God, healer of body and soul.

Heal me, O Lord, and I shall be healed; save me,
and I shall be saved: for thou art my praise.

JEREMIAH 17:14 KJV

"In sickness and in health," the traditional wedding vow declares, and
God declares the same to you. Your sickness may diminish your ability to
enjoy life right now, but it cannot diminish God's presence in your life or
affect His control over all aspects of your well-being. Pray for His healing
then wait on Him, confident in His solemn, unbreakable vow to remain
with you "in sickness and in health" forever.

Indecision

Preserve sound judgment and discernment, do not
let them out of your sight; they will be life for you,
an ornament to grace your neck.

PROVERBS 3:21–22

You don't want to make the wrong decision, so you weigh the pros and cons in your mind over and over, spending sleepless nights wondering what to do. Now would be a good time to stop tossing and turning and put the matter in God's hands. Only He knows the outcome of all possible scenarios. Study His Word on the topic, bring to Him your best thinking on the matter, and open yourself to the guidance of His Spirit. Then make your decision with certainty and confidence.

....

....

....

....

....

....

....

....

....

....

....

> I will praise the LORD, who counsels me;
> even at night my heart instructs me.
>
> PSALM 16:7

When you're faced with a decision, you have a wise counselor in God's Word. Open the Bible, because in it God has revealed His will and His guidelines for the lives of His people, a necessary foundation for any good decision. You also have a wise counselor in His Holy Spirit. Let Him teach you how to pray about the decision you need to make. When you do these things, you will discover His answer.

Intolerance

What does the LORD require of you? To act justly and to
love mercy and to walk humbly with your God.

MICAH 6:8

When you find yourself easily irritated by others, God wants you to look within yourself. Take stock of your feelings and make an honest assessment of your attitude. With the help of the Holy Spirit, turn away from intolerance. Let His Spirit work in you a heart of compassion, a heart willing to forgive, to accept differences, and to walk humbly with your God.

He who despises his neighbor sins,
but blessed is he who is kind to the needy.

Even in the most conscientious heart, intolerance finds a place to fester. It can raise its ugly head with one disapproving thought of "those people." Invite the Holy Spirit into your heart to banish any feelings of intolerance you may harbor. Ask Him to open your spiritual eyes so you will see God's presence in others, finding Him reflected in their eyes as He is reflected in yours. Then think of "those people" accordingly—as children of God created in His image.

Laughter

[God] will yet fill your mouth with laughter
and your lips with shouts of joy.

JOB 8:21

The old saying might ring true for you right now: "Laugh and the world laughs with you; weep and you weep alone." Yet you know you're not alone when you weep. God remains at your side with the comfort of His peace, relief, and, yes, laughter. Seem impossible? Not with God. Not when you immerse yourself in His presence today and bathe in the certainty of a better tomorrow. Let Him fill your life with laughter!

....

....

....

....

....

....

....

....

....

My. . .sisters, be full of joy in the Lord.

PHILIPPIANS 3:1 NCV

*I*f you have placed your hope and faith in God, you have every reason to be happy. You know who you are and whose you are. You have set your heart on doing His will, and you hold to His promises to protect and preserve you in any situation you may face in life. Take a moment to thank Him for bringing you into the light of His love, and cultivate a spirit of genuine joy.

Leadership

**The greatest among you should be like the youngest,
and the one who rules like the one who serves.**

LUKE 22:26

*N*o matter what your role in life, you're a leader. Either your words and actions lead people toward goodness and virtue, or your conduct turns people away. For this reason, God gives this advice: "Lead by being as happy to walk with the weakest as with the strongest. Lead by being as happy to serve others in an unnoticed, unsung capacity as to take center stage." Follow the example of Christ, who comforted even His enemies.

Follow my example, as I follow the example of Christ.

1 Corinthians 11:1

*I*f you want to learn about leadership, look at the life of Jesus Christ. Though the Son of God, He did not use His status to intimidate others or amass power, but to serve both the powerful and the weak. This is the example Jesus has set for you. Never shirk your responsibility to those beneath you in authority, education, or social status. Instead, do everything you can to bless the lives of others.

Loneliness

A father to the fatherless, a defender of widows, is God in
his holy dwelling. God sets the lonely in families.

PSALM 68:5–6

*N*o one has come to take the place of the one no longer in your life, and
you're not sure anyone really could. You ache with loneliness. These days
are tough, and they're not days God wants to prolong. He sends people—
relatives, friends, even strangers sometimes—to lift loneliness from you
and bring you into the company and companionship of others. Ask Him
to open your eyes and heart to those He sends to comfort you.

....

....

....

....

....

....

....

....

....

....

[God said,] "Never will I leave you;
never will I forsake you."

HEBREWS 13:5

*Y*ou know what it's like to feel lonely in a crowd, because you feel that way right now. Even though many people surround you, you realize not one of them truly understands what you're going through. But do you believe God understands you—truly understands? He does, you know. And He yearns for you to let Him fill your loneliness with His presence and the fullness of His compassion and care.

Loss

I consider everything a loss compared to the surpassing
greatness of knowing Christ Jesus my Lord.

PHILIPPIANS 3:8

*Y*ou've lost something or someone that meant the world to you, and
now all you can see is a big hole where your future used to be. If you let
God step into that big hole, you'll see Him fill it up, spill out, and tower
over it. Where emptiness scared you moments before, abundance invites
you now. God asks you to come with Him while He walks you safely
through your sorrow and makes of it a renewed tomorrow and a new
future.

> "Whoever finds his life will lose it, and whoever loses his life for my sake will find it."

MATTHEW 10:39

Perhaps you have never told anyone how many of your dreams and desires you have given up for the sake of doing God's will. When it comes to sacrifice, few answer His call, but you did. He knows, and because you have suffered the calculated loss of your own plans and agenda, you will find your gains to be more than you could have imagined possible.

Marriage

This is the message you heard from the beginning:
We should love one another.

1 JOHN 3:11

*E*very marriage has its rocky patches, but it's possible that in yours a few rocky patches have begun to merge into a road of gutted potholes. Have you and your spouse prayed about your marriage? Ask the Holy Spirit to come into your lives, and let Him show you where the love lies among all those stones. Allow God, the God of love, who created marriage to be a blessing to the two of you, smooth the path ahead. He is willing and able to help.

Understand this, my dear brothers and sisters: You must all be quick to listen, slow to speak, and slow to get angry. Human anger does not produce the righteousness God desires.

JAMES 1:19–20 NLT

*T*ime has eroded mutual respect, and habit has taken away the simple courtesies and small surprises that once made your relationship special. This is not what you want for your marriage; it's not what God wants, either. Invite Him to help both of you commit yourselves to needed changes in how you treat each other. Begin with your own heart, where the God of love waits to comfort, renew, restore, and bless your married life.

Ministry

He has made us competent as ministers of a new
covenant—not of the letter but of the Spirit;
for the letter kills, but the Spirit gives life.

2 CORINTHIANS 3:6

*C*aring for and comforting others is a profound privilege. With God's
Spirit at work in you, let your everyday words and actions comfort and bless
others just as God has comforted and blessed you. Your ministry makes you
a love-sharer rather than a lawgiver. Maybe you feel you have nothing to
share with others, but you do. God loves you, and knowing that enables you
to love others.

_____

_____

_____

_____

_____

_____

_____

_____

_____

_____

"When you give a banquet, invite the poor, the crippled,
the lame, the blind, and you will be blessed. Although
they cannot repay you, you will be repaid at the
resurrection of the righteous."

LUKE 14:13–14

Complaints and criticisms hurt, and you might just as soon serve only those people who know how to say thank you. Rest assured God hears you. He knows what it's like to shower people with blessings only to have them congratulate themselves for their good fortune. Yet He continues to bless, and He invites you to follow Him in His ministry. You will hear His comforting thank-you, because He knows.

Mistakes

Happy is the person whose sins are forgiven,
whose wrongs are pardoned.

PSALM 32:1 NCV

Admitting guilt isn't easy for anyone. It's uncomfortable and embarrassing. But when we take full responsibility for our sins, God can bring us comfort and confidence. You, too, have made mistakes; we all have. The good news is that we aren't doomed by the mistakes we've made—not at all. With God there is room for pardon. Tell Him about your mistakes, and let Him help you find a new beginning.

....

....

....

....

....

....

....

....

....

....

[Jesus said,] "Forgive us our sins, as we have
forgiven those who sin against us."

MATTHEW 6:12 NLT

The weaknesses, mistakes, and sins of others affect your life,
sometimes bringing serious and lasting harm to you and those you
love. You have a right to feel angry, but God offers a better alternative.
He urges you to forgive, because forgiveness is the only way to prevent
bitterness from taking root in your soul. Compare the "right" of
bitterness and the privilege of forgiveness. Choose to forgive.

Money

My God will meet all your needs according
to his glorious riches in Christ Jesus.

PHILIPPIANS 4:19

God knows how you feel when money runs out at the end of the month.
He has compassion on you in your concern for those dependent on your
ability to meet their needs. Let Him remind you of something: He's in
the need-meeting business, too. The God who long ago met your most
pressing spiritual need does not abandon you in this, your earthly need.
Take all your needs to Him in prayer, for He hears and answers.

> Keep your lives free from the love of money and be
> content with what you have.

HEBREWS 13:5

God doesn't ask you to live without money, but He warns you against the love of money. He wants to free you from the spiritually corrosive sins of greed and envy, and He wants to release you from the bondage of a never-ending list of must-haves. Turn from a love of money and the things it can buy. Ask His Spirit in you to become your most cherished possession, and you will find a rich contentment in everything.

Motives

Serve him with wholehearted devotion and with a willing mind, for the LORD searches every heart and understands every motive behind the thoughts.

I CHRONICLES 28:9

We claim publicly we're asking for no reward but seek acclaim privately when no reward comes our way. If you find yourself harboring offense, check the motives behind your charitable acts. God already has. Ask Him to replace selfish motives with selfless ones and to instill in you a spirit of compassion, kindness, and generosity. On the outside, you'll continue doing the good things you've been doing. On the inside, you'll be doing them for the right reason.

Pursue righteousness, faith, love and peace, along with those who call on the Lord out of a pure heart.

2 TIMOTHY 2:22

*T*hough your motives are pure toward others, you will encounter those whose hearts aren't pure, and it hurts to find out someone has used you for their own purposes. When that happens—and it almost certainly will at one time or another—take comfort in God. You can be sure that even when others are untrue, God never wavers. He is always thinking of you, putting your best interests first.

Obedience

The proof that we love God comes when we keep his
commandments and they are not at all troublesome.

1 JOHN 5:3 MSG

*I*f you have broken one of God's commandments and now see the
reason why He put that commandment there in the first place, you've
learned an important lesson. Why repeat it? He has given you His
commandments not to burden you with outdated rules and undue
regulations but for your physical, emotional, and spiritual well-being.
Embrace all His commandments and obey them, and you will live in the
full freedom He intends for you.

....

....

....

....

....

....

....

....

....

....

If anyone obeys his word, God's love is truly made
complete in him. This is how we know we are in him.

1 JOHN 2:5

*I*f a camera were to record your every word and action today, what
would those watching the film learn about you? Would they be able to
see that you love God, that you belong to Him? God is pure and holy, and
when we strive to live by the commandments He's given us with sincere
and humble hearts, others see the resemblance. They can tell that we
are His children.

Obstacles

God will strengthen you with his own great power
so that you will not give up when troubles come,
but you will be patient.

COLOSSIANS 1:11 NCV

*P*erhaps you are facing a mountain in your life—a circumstance so tall and fierce that you have given up before you even started. You're sure there is no way around it, no solution, no hope for you. Take comfort in the fact that you are not facing your mountain alone. God is with you. While your strength is small, God's is great. He may lead you around, over, or help you carve a path right through the middle. Take His hand and somehow you will overcome.

_____

_____

_____

_____

_____

_____

_____

_____

_____

_____

He will not let you be defeated.
He who guards you never sleeps.

PSALM 121:3 NCV

*D*iscrimination. Ridicule. Mockery. The obstacles towering in front of you look insurmountable. From your vantage point, if you were to stray just a little from God's way, you could get around the problem and minimize its effect on your life. But consider God's vantage point. He has traveled this way before you, and He knows there are no safe detours. Trust Him to lead you to the other side the right way—His way.

Offenses

**I have swept away your offenses like a cloud,
your sins like the morning mist.**

ISAIAH 44:22

*I*f you have ever watched the morning sun burn away the fog, recall the image when you come before God in prayer. Any offense against God you have ever committed—either intentionally or unintentionally—has been burned away in the light of His forgiveness. Offenses no longer cover you, and guilt no longer shrouds your heart. God has done this for you because He loves you. Respond in joyous thanksgiving today!

Love makes up for all offenses.

PROVERBS 10:12 NLT

False love denies offenses and lives an illusion, but real love acknowledges the offense—and covers it with a compassionate, forgiving heart. Blind love says "nothing happened" and hides in the shadows, but real love says "I forgive you" and begins a new day. What kind of love do you show toward others? Pray for real love, the kind of love God has first shown you. Real love covers. Real love forgives. Real love lasts for eternity.

Past

This is what God says. . . "Forget about what's happened; don't keep going over old history."

ISAIAH 43:16,18 MSG

A parent, a child, a spouse just can't forget—and won't let you forget, either. Or maybe it's the other way around. In either case, the past is poisoning the present. Invite God into the picture and ask Him to help you apply His antidote to this cycle of unhealthy and hurtful arguments and accusations. His antidote? Repentance. Forgiveness. Commitment to put the past behind you. God's comfort thrives even in the midst of conflict.

_Forgetting the past and straining toward what is ahead,
I keep trying to reach the goal and get the prize for which
God called me through Christ to the life above._

PHILIPPIANS 3:13–14 NCV

Your past continues to haunt you. Why wouldn't it? What you did and who you were back then leave nothing but shameful memories. God was there, too, and He saw everything. He is here now, however, and He sees an older, wiser, and completely forgiven child of God. His forgiveness gives you the go-ahead to continue with your life, renewed and energized, with your focus on Him and a new eternity.

Patience

Patience is better than strength.
PROVERBS 16:32 NCV

I'm not a patient person!" You've heard it said, and perhaps you've even said it yourself. Unfortunately, the statement supports a false idea about patience. Rather than an inborn personality trait given only to some, patience is a gift of the Holy Spirit worked in the hearts of those who love Him. Godly patience allows you to respond to life's trying situations with serenity and self-control, sure evidence of your continuing walk with God.

_____

_____

_____

_____

_____

_____

_____

_____

_____

_____

Let us not become weary in doing good, for at the proper time we will reap a harvest if we do not give up.

GALATIANS 6:9

Things aren't happening quickly enough, and you're feeling frustrated. Pause for a moment and compare your timetable with God's timetable. Evidently they don't match! Instead of fighting against His gracious will, put your trust in it. Let Him unfold the hours, days, and years to you in His own time. His time is, without fail, the right time. Learn from Him the difference godly patience can work in your heart, mind, and spirit.

Peace

You, LORD, give true peace to those who depend on you, because they trust you.

ISAIAH 26:3 NCV

Daily stress, nagging worries, and ceaseless squabbles make you long for a place—an hour—of peace. You don't need to look for a serene spot, however, and you don't need to arrange a special time to rest your heart in God's peace. He has it for you right now, right where you are. Give God all those things that drive out peace—name them, hand them over, and don't grab them back again! Then take comfort in the peace He has for you.

....

....

....

....

....

....

....

....

....

....

A heart at peace gives life to the body.

PROVERBS 14:30

Without question, mind and body are linked. God made us that way! His gift of spiritual peace not only soothes a troubled mind by replacing worry with trust, fear with faith, but it also permits a tired, nervous body to get a good night's sleep. Let God fight the battles taking place in your mind, and let your heart rest in His peace. Commit yourself to Him, the healer and restorer of life.

Perfection

All have sinned and fall short of the glory of God,
and are justified freely by his grace through
the redemption that came by Christ Jesus.

ROMANS 3:23–24

*Y*ou may have spent years trying to reach perfection, but perfection remains out of your grasp. Your futile striving has landed you right where God wants you—in His arms, admitting your utter lack of power to make yourself perfect. Now you're ready to hear what He has done for you. Long ago, He declared you perfect by sending Jesus Christ to remove your imperfections. Only He has the power to do so, and He did.

....

....

....

....

....

....

....

....

....

....

To all perfection I see a limit;
but your commands are boundless.

PSALM 119:96

You may look with awe at the perfection of the stars on a dark, clear night, and melt in joy at the sight of a newborn's perfect eyes, ears, fingers, and toes. With the same sense of wonder, consider God's commandments, spoken by God for your daily guidance and eternal good. He sets His commandments before you this day, inviting you to meditate on the boundless perfection of His words and take them, in their entirety, into your heart.

Persecution

Who shall separate us from the love of Christ? Shall trouble
or hardship or persecution or famine or nakedness or
danger or sword? . . . No, in all these things we are more
than conquerors through him who loved us.

ROMANS 8:35, 37

As the Holy Spirit immerses your soul in the sweetness of God's love,
your attitude and behavior undergo noticeable changes. Now you're
more discerning in your choices and more thoughtful about what you say
and do. Some people, however, will clamor for the "old you" back, even
resorting to name-calling and slander when you refuse. Don't let their
persecution sway you, but call on God, whose strength and comfort are
yours in all situations you face.

_____

_____

_____

_____

_____

_____

_____

_____

_____

_____

> Everyone who wants to live a godly life
> in Christ Jesus will be persecuted.
>
> 2 TIMOTHY 3:12

*Y*ou know how it is when someone is successful; many times people will applaud them publicly while saying and doing hurtful things behind their backs. When you begin to live a life of peace and joy as God's child, there will be those who will smile to your face but secretly resent you for it. When that happens, you must forgive. Use those situations as opportunities to let others know that they can have what you have. All they have to do is ask.

Perspective

"My thoughts are not your thoughts, neither are your ways
my ways," declares the LORD. "As the heavens are higher
than the earth, so are my ways higher than your ways and
my thoughts than your thoughts."

ISAIAH 55:8–9

*W*e plan, God laughs." While the saying gets a chuckle, we're usually
not chuckling when our plans go awry. But step back and look at the
situation from another perspective—God's perspective. He sees your
future as clearly as He sees your past and present, and He knows how to
get you from here to there. Ask the Holy Spirit to help you look from God's
perspective—and laugh with the joy of knowing you remain under His
watchful care!

Do not be shaped by this world; instead be changed within by a new way of thinking. Then you will be able to decide what God wants for you; you will know what is good and pleasing to him and what is perfect.

ROMANS 12:2 NCV

When you live for the moment, your perspective focuses on what will bring you instant pleasure and immediate gratification. The Holy Spirit has opened to you a deeper, longer, and broader perspective—an eternal perspective. Now you're disposed to put aside selfish desires in favor of godly choices, and you're willing to weigh the spiritual consequences of your actions. Practice seeing with an eternal perspective every day, and prepare to notice eternal results.

Pleasing God

Our only goal is to please God.
2 CORINTHIANS 5:9 NCV

*W*hen you have a specific goal in mind, you take every opportunity and use every resource available to you to reach your goal. The goal of living a God-pleasing life is no different. Look for opportunities in your day to do those things you know God wants you to do. Use the resources you have on hand right now to strengthen your faith, increase your understanding of His Word, and serve others with Christlike love in your heart.

Beloved, if our heart condemn us not, then have we
confidence toward God. And whatsoever we ask,
we receive of him, because we keep his commandments,
and do those things that are pleasing in his sight.

1 JOHN 3:21–22 KJV

*I*f you have been waiting to get your life in order before you focus on pleasing God, God has a happy surprise for you. God has put your life in order through the earthly ministry of Jesus. As His forgiven child, respond in genuine joy and gratitude by living to please Him. Worship Him, obey His commandments, and show compassion on others. By focusing on pleasing God, you will find your life in God-pleasing order.

Potential

I have filled [you] with the Spirit of God, with skill,
ability and knowledge in all kinds of crafts.

EXODUS 31:3

*H*ave you reached your full potential? If you're still breathing, you haven't! God has blessed you with a wide range of talents for you to tap throughout your life. Enrich every stage of your life by following your interests, broadening your knowledge, and developing your abilities. You will be surprised at the variety of God-given gifts you possess—and experience the sheer enjoyment of embracing your potential.

....

....

....

....

....

....

....

....

....

....

> In [God] you have been enriched in every way—
> in all your speaking and in all your knowledge.
>
> I CORINTHIANS 1:5

Ask God to show you where you are not using the potential your faith has given you. Consider the things you already know about God and His commandments, and use your knowledge to introduce others to God's love. List your abilities—you have more than you think!—and consciously use them to serve others. Use your Spirit-given potential to walk as an effective, exciting, and powerful woman of God.

Prayer

"You will call upon me and come and pray to me,
and I will listen to you. You will seek me and find
me when you seek me with all your heart."

JEREMIAH 29:12–13

You may have heard many differing opinions on the subject of prayer. What God says about prayer, however, is simple. When you pray— whether kneeling, sitting, or standing; whether in time-tested words or in your own words—He hears you. He responds in a way designed to increase your faith and develop a strong relationship with Him. Continue to pray and pray faithfully, because through prayer, God offers you the comfort of daily conversation between your heart and His.

_____

_____

_____

_____

_____

_____

_____

_____

_____

_____

The LORD hath heard the voice of my weeping.
The LORD hath heard my supplication;
the LORD will receive my prayer.

PSALM 6:8–9 KJV

When you don't receive what you've prayed for, it's easy to conclude God is telling you no. Not so! He has promised to hear your prayers, but are you listening for His answer? If He chooses not to give you exactly what you have prayed for, He has chosen something better for you. If He chooses to remain silent today, He is encouraging you to continue praying, placing your trust in Him and His wisdom.

Priorities

Fear God and obey his commands,
for this is everyone's duty.

ECCLESIASTES 12:13 NLT

Knowing God gives you a new perspective on your work, family life, and friendships. You see these God-given blessings for what they are, and you want to tend to them mindfully and well. Like a broad umbrella, however, God stands over and above you and all He has given you. Never let anything in your life take priority over God, who shelters you with His continuing guidance, comfort, and care.

> Seek his will in all you do, and he
> will show you which path to take.

PROVERBS 3:6 NLT

*F*inancial troubles, medical issues, relationship problems, and similar difficulties tend to occupy first place in thoughts, time, and energy. Yet this is exactly the time your priorities need to be in order! If you allow a crisis to dominate, anxiety continues to consume you, and you lose sight of the help, strength, and solace you have in God. Whether things are going smoothly or not so smoothly, make sure God stays first in your life.

Protection

I've run to you for dear life. I'm hiding out under
your wings until the hurricane blows over.

PSALM 57:1 MSG

*W*hen bad things happen, we tend to wonder, *Isn't God supposed
to protect us from disaster?* Rest assured your God knows and cares
about what is taking place in your life, and His arms of comfort and
consolation are there to enfold you in His love. All the while, His Holy
Spirit is working in you to guard and keep your soul from anything that
would threaten your eternal salvation. Hold firmly to God, and discover
your immediate solace and your ultimate safety in Him.

....

....

....

....

....

....

....

....

....

....

The eternal God is your refuge,
and underneath are the everlasting arms.

DEUTERONOMY 33:27

God's commandments always work to protect your soul and very often your mind, emotions, and body from danger. He sets His guidelines under you to keep you away from anything capable of stealing the good in your life and covering you with guilt, pain, and regret. Pray for a deeper appreciation of the refuge He has set for you in His commandments and will for your life.

Provision

[God] gives food to those who fear him;
he always remembers his covenant.

PSALM 111:5 NLT

We serve a God of miracles, and sometimes miracles come in the simplest provisions—food enough for the next meal, a warm coat for your child, a place to sleep at night. When the checkbook gets low and the bills are stacking up, He is there to point you to help, to see that you and yours have the basic needs of daily living. Thank Him for both the small miracles and the great ones.

> God will generously provide all you need.
> Then you will always have everything you need
> and plenty left over to share with others.

2 CORINTHIANS 9:8 NLT

In a culture replete with consumer goods, the line between needs and wants tends to blur not only in ads and commercials, but in our thoughts as well. God's mind, however, is clear on the subject of needs and wants—He knows the difference. Trust Him to give you those things He knows you need, and give thanks to Him for all He provides. If you think about it, you'll realize He has given you plenty to share with others, too!

Purpose

We are God's workmanship, created in Christ Jesus to do
good works, which God prepared in advance for us to do.

EPHESIANS 2:10

*S*ome people say life is merely a meaningless accident of nature.
Perhaps the idea has entered your mind and thoughts, too. If so, you
understand why God in His Word declares repeatedly the value He places
on human life. He created you out of His eternal love, and He has made
you who you are and placed you where you are for His divine purpose.
Open your heart and spirit to take hold of the great purpose God has for
your life.

....

....

....

....

....

....

....

....

....

....

We constantly pray for you, that our God may count you worthy of his calling, and that by his power he may fulfill every good purpose of yours and every act prompted by your faith.

2 THESSALONIANS 1:11

*I*f you could plan the course of your children's lives, would you doom them to failure and despair? Of course not. You love your children. Your plans for them would all be good. Your heavenly Father feels the same about you. And He does have the power to set in place a plan and purpose for your life. You can be certain that His will includes only the best for you—the best of joy, of love, of peace, of abundance, of success.

Questions

On the day I called, You answered me;
You made me bold with strength in my soul.

PSALM 138:3 NASB

"What is this?" "Where are we now?" "How come this is this way?"
One thing children know how to do is ask questions. Mothers know,
however, that their children might not be ready or able to hear the
answers to all their questions, so they answer the ones they can and tuck
the others away. Your heavenly Father hears your questions, all of them.
But He doesn't give you all the answers at once. Trust Him to know what
you can handle. Answer in faith.

_____

_____

_____

_____

_____

_____

_____

_____

_____

"Call to me and I will answer you and tell you great
and unsearchable things you do not know."

JEREMIAH 33:3

*I*f you have ever worked with children, you know they will sometimes ask a question but not listen to your answer. As God's child, avoid doing the same thing. Pose your questions to God, and then listen to His answer. You may not like what you hear—it may be difficult to accept or sound unreasonable to you. Ask the Holy Spirit to deepen your understanding and give you the power to accept even the most difficult of God's unsearchable answers.

Respect

A kindhearted woman gains respect.

PROVERBS 11:16

*W*hen you consistently show kindness and caring for others, sincerely honoring their humanity, their work, and their rights, you gain their respect. They cannot help but notice the respect you offer to everyone, from the lowliest person to the highest, from the youngest to the oldest, from the weakest to the most powerful. Ask the Holy Spirit to help you show heartfelt respect to others, because this is the way you gain respect in return.

_____

_____

_____

_____

_____

_____

_____

_____

_____

Make it your ambition to lead a quiet life, to mind your own business
and to work with your hands, just as we told you, so that your daily
life may win the respect of outsiders and so that you will not be
dependent on anybody.

1 THESSALONIANS 4:11–12

*W*ho you are in public and in private shapes your character and
the perception people have about you. Do you consistently act in a way
deserving of others' respect? Do your words and actions put others in
the best light? Ask the Holy Spirit to show you what you could change
to heighten the respect others have for you and to build respect for the
presence of God in your life.

Responsibility

To do what is right and just is more
acceptable to the LORD than sacrifice.

PROVERBS 21:3

*W*hether or not God ever calls you to make a huge personal sacrifice
for Him, He definitely calls you to take on the responsibilities He has
placed in front of you. These responsibilities may not differ in essence
from anyone else's responsibilities, but your willing and uncomplaining
acceptance of them marks you as His child. Perform them to the best of
your ability, and in all you do, do the right thing.

Pay careful attention to your own work, for then you will get the satisfaction of a job well done, and you won't need to compare yourself to anyone else. For we are each responsible for our own conduct.

GALATIANS 6:4–5 NLT

God has loaded you with more responsibilities than you can handle—or so you think! In fact, He never gives you responsibilities without also giving you the strength to manage your tasks well. When you feel overwhelmed, don't focus on getting out from under your responsibilities. Instead ask the Holy Spirit to build you up in faith and attentiveness so you can carry your own load with dignity and a true appreciation of your God-given abilities.

Rest

[Jesus said]: "Are you tired? Worn out? Burned out on religion? Come to me. Get away with me and you'll recover your life. I'll show you how to take a real rest."

MATTHEW 11:28 MSG

*Y*ou know how it is. Busy schedules and pressure to perform crowd in on every side. But God never intended for you to be spent and weary in body and soul. Not only does He permit us to rest; He insists on it. Ask God to show you where you can open up some time to rest your body and nourish your soul, close your eyes, and relax in His comforting arms.

....

....

....

....

....

....

....

....

....

....

Rest in the LORD, and wait patiently for Him.

PSALM 37:7 NKJV

*Y*ou need more than rest for your body. Your mind and emotions also need to be renewed. God understands how difficult it is to step away when so many people are depending on you. Ask Him to help you find respites in the storms of life, special times, however brief, when you can rest your body and soul. Listen as He says, "Come, My weary daughter, and I will give you rest."

Restoration

"I will restore you to health and heal your wounds,"
declares the LORD.

JEREMIAH 30:17

*H*ave you prayed many times for God's restoring hand in your life, and yet you can't seem to get over those memories and emotions that cause you so much pain? God's healing sometimes happens overnight, but most often it takes time. Take comfort in knowing that each day in some small way, He is bringing you through, giving you strength, creating for you a future based on His love.

The God of all grace, who called you to his eternal glory
in Christ, after you have suffered a little while, will himself
restore you and make you strong, firm and steadfast.

1 PETER 5:10

*N*o matter how low your sufferings may have brought you, God works
to lift you up and build you up. He is a God who takes no pleasure in
seeing you broken in body or in spirit, but He takes great pleasure in
restoring you and filling you with more of His spiritual gifts of patience,
faith, and strength of character. Lift your eyes to God's unchangeable
promise to heal you, and keep your trust in Him.

Reward

[Jesus said,] "Blessed are you when people insult you, persecute you and falsely say all kinds of evil against you because of me. Rejoice and be glad, because great is your reward in heaven."

MATTHEW 5:11–12

Though it seems noble to say, "I'm not doing this for a reward," Jesus promises a sure and certain reward to those who follow Him in obedience. His promise works to comfort you when your commitment to Him makes you the object of insult, ridicule, or slander. Don't let these things take away your peace, but instead be glad. Let insults remind you: Great is your reward in heaven.

You know that the Lord will reward
everyone for whatever good he does.

EPHESIANS 6:8

Through the ministry of Jesus Christ, God has done for you what you could never do for yourself—secure your salvation. He has satisfied your greatest need. Now His Holy Spirit working in you prompts you to do the things He invites His followers to do. That is, show compassion, give practical assistance to those in need, and share your spiritual wisdom and understanding. He even offers you an incentive—eternal reward from your Lord and God.

Service

There are different kinds of service, but the same Lord.

I CORINTHIANS 12:5

*E*ven after you commit yourself to following God's will, jealousy can creep into your heart. You notice her work gets so much more recognition than yours and her gifts seem so much greater. God would have you turn from the temptation to compare your work with anyone else's. Both of you in your different roles serve the same God. Put your confidence in Him as you serve Him and others in every way open to you.

_____

_____

_____

_____

_____

_____

_____

_____

_____

_____

[Jesus said,] "Whoever serves me must follow me;
and where I am, my servant also will be. My Father
will honor the one who serves me."

JOHN 12:26

$\mathcal{F}$ollowing Jesus requires you to serve others wherever you are. Never
for a moment wait for other circumstances, a more convenient time, a
later date! The moment you commit yourself to following Jesus Christ,
you give yourself to serving others by showing compassion and kindness,
by offering help and counsel, by bringing His love wherever you are right
now. Pray for His Spirit to open your eyes to see opportunities
to serve Him.

Spiritual Struggle

Put on the full armor of God so that you can take your stand against the devil's schemes. For our struggle is not against flesh and blood, but against the rulers, against the authorities, against the powers of this dark world and against the spiritual forces of evil in the heavenly realms.

EPHESIANS 6:11–12

*Y*ou cannot fight temptation on your own. Deadly spiritual forces work to pull you away from God and into the grip of sin, turmoil, and despair. Pray for a realistic awareness of the forces fighting against you, and let the Holy Spirit equip you for the struggle. Fill your mind and heart with His Word, dedicate yourself to listening only to the still, small voice of God inside you, and rely on His power and strength.

Pursue righteousness, godliness, faith, love, endurance and
gentleness. Fight the good fight of the faith.

1 TIMOTHY 6:11–12

Through your faith, God's Spirit has put into your heart the vision of
His will for your life. It's like a precious gift inside you, building you
up and giving you the desire and motivation you need to fight for your
spiritual life. Keep doing the right thing, continue learning, and persist
in praying that your faith will grow and strengthen in the struggle.
Spiritual warfare is happening because you've moved away from the grip
of wickedness and into the arms of God. Give thanks!

Starting Over

This is what the LORD says—your Redeemer, the Holy One
of Israel. . ."I am about to do something new. See, I have
already begun! Do you not see it?"

ISAIAH 43:14, 19 NLT

When the Holy Spirit brought you to faith in Jesus Christ, your life
started over. You may or may not have realized it at the time, and since
then you might have slid right back into doing things the same old way
and thinking the same old thoughts. Your new life in Christ, however, is
not a onetime event. It happens each time you come to Him and ask for
renewal and refreshment. Seek Him, and start over again today.

Create in me a pure heart, God,
and make my spirit right again.

PSALM 51:10 NCV

The psalmist had strayed so far from God's will for his life that he
dropped to his knees and prayed for a whole new heart and spirit. If you
have strayed, you can join the psalmist in his plea. Ask God to give you a
clean heart, a restored spirit, and a chance to walk with Him again. Trust
in Him to forgive you, and you will see the miracle of a brand-new life.

Strength

I can do everything through him who gives me strength.

PHILIPPIANS 4:13

*H*as a new opportunity opened for you? Maybe after thinking and praying about it, you feel drawn to take on the project, but a nagging doubt holds you back. Are you strong enough? If you keep looking at your own strength, you will pass on the opportunity. If instead you look to God and realize it's His strength He's offering, you can take on the challenge with confidence. In Him you have great strength!

The Lord is faithful, and he will strengthen
and protect you from the evil one.

2 THESSALONIANS 3:3

God never expects you to hold on to your faith by your own strength.
He knows the weakness of all human hearts, and He knows all about the
temptations you deal with every day. With His own strength, God will
defend you! Ask the Holy Spirit to give you His strength and power, so
you will exercise your spiritual muscles and move beyond your frailty.
Where you are weak, God is strong.

Suffering

I consider that our present sufferings are not worth
comparing with the glory that will be revealed in us.

ROMANS 8:18

*W*hen you suffer, it's hard to think of anything except your suffering, and that's why God provides something else to think about, something to balance the pain you are feeling now. Despite the circumstances of your suffering, open your spiritual eyes to how He is using the situation to reveal to you and others His presence and His power. To break through the darkness of suffering, take your hope and comfort from the shining light of His unfailing love.

_____

_____

_____

_____

_____

_____

_____

_____

_____

Those who suffer as God wants should
trust their souls to the faithful Creator.

1 PETER 4:19 NCV

It's possible that through no fault of your own, you are enduring the
pain of grief, despair, and hopelessness. God understands the depth
of your suffering, even your anger that life should treat you so unfairly.
Allow His Spirit to use your suffering as a starting point for His healing
as He restores hope and instills His strength in you. Entrust yourself to
your faithful God, for in Him you have life, peace, and comfort.

Surrender

[Jesus said,] "If you try to hang on to your life, you will lose it. But if you give up your life for my sake and for the sake of the Good News, you will save it."

MARK 8:35 NLT

*Y*ou may have thought about the concept of surrendering yourself to God, but you've hesitated because you want to be who you are—not a puppet of someone else. Don't worry! After all, God is the one who created you to be the unique woman you are. He has no intention of tampering with that. His goal is just to offer stability in your emotions and thought life and to enhance your talents and abilities. Surrender to the hand of God means fulfillment of your deepest God-given desires.

_____

_____

_____

_____

_____

_____

_____

_____

_____

Give yourselves completely to God. Stand against the devil,
and the devil will run from you. Come near to God,
and God will come near to you.

JAMES 4:7–8 NCV

Sometimes when we aren't entirely convinced we want to go all out
for God, we try to keep Him at a safe distance. Yet to go all out for Him
is what God is asking each of us to do. He knows how hesitance keeps us
vulnerable to the pull of doubt, the fear of life, and the pain of reverting
to our old ways. Let Him close the distance between you. You will be
amazed by how comforting it can be to be fully surrendered to Him.

Temptation

Because [Jesus] himself suffered when he was tempted,
he is able to help those who are being tempted.

HEBREWS 2:18

Jesus has passed this way ahead of you. In His humanity, He was tempted and He knows firsthand its power and pull. He has compassion on the weakness of human flesh, and He is not ashamed to travel with you in your struggle. He wants you to live free, without the tentacles and restrictions of destructive behaviors and unhealthy desires. The challenge is great, but He has promised to walk with you, comforting and strengthening you every step of the way.

No test or temptation that comes your way is beyond the course of what others have had to face. All you need to remember is that God will never let you down; he'll never let you be pushed past your limit; he'll always be there to help you come through it.

1 CORINTHIANS 10:13 MSG

*Y*our faith and commitment to God will be tested, and often tests come in the form of deeply personal, private, even foul temptation. Don't be fooled into thinking you're the only one ever tempted in this way. You're not! Take the temptation to God in prayer, asking Him to lift its burden from you. No matter how long you may struggle against it, you have the God-given strength to resist it. And because God is there to help you, you will never walk alone.

Time

There is a right time and a right way for everything.

ECCLESIASTES 8:6 NCV

*P*ure and simple, time is a gift. Each second, minute, hour, and day is yours to use as you please. *Not so fast,* you might be thinking. *All my time is filled with work and responsibilities and taking care of other people.* That's true, your time might be dictated by other choices you have made, but it is still yours. Ask God to help you squeeze in some time for yourself. He'll show you where to find it.

_____

_____

_____

_____

_____

_____

_____

_____

_____

_____

> [God] has made everything beautiful in its time.
> He has also set eternity in the hearts of men; yet they
> cannot fathom what God has done from beginning to end.

ECCLESIASTES 3:11

*Y*ou wonder, sometimes with great anxiety, what time will bring. Let God put your mind at ease. Remember, He was present at the beginning and will be present at the end. He knows everything that has happened or will happen in between, including all the days and years of your life. Entrust the time you've been given to God, and do not fear for the future. His hand is on eternity.

Trials

When you have many kinds of troubles, you should be full of joy, because you know that these troubles test your faith, and this will give you patience. Let your patience show itself perfectly in what you do. Then you will be perfect and complete and will have everything you need.

JAMES 1:2–4 NCV

God never discounts the pain you go through during life's difficult trials, but He always finds a way to use your pain for your advantage. Through trials, He reveals to you the quality of your faith, so you can see where your weaknesses are and take these things to Him in prayer. Without trials, you might never realize the deep comfort of His presence or the penetrating glow of His eternal love.

....

....

....

....

....

....

....

....

....

> God blesses those who patiently endure testing and temptation. Afterward they will receive the crown of life that God has promised to those who love him.

JAMES 1:12 NLT

*G*od permits trials to pit your faith against life's harsh realities. It is the only venue in which you are able to see His power and appreciate His unwavering commitment to you. You might know that God loves you, but the reality comes in the difficult times. You might acknowledge that He is wise, but you won't appreciate it fully until you have seen Him guide you to safer ground. Rejoice in your trials, for they help you learn who God is in your life.

Trust

Trust the LORD with all your heart,
and don't depend on your own understanding.

PROVERBS 3:5 NCV

You might have been taught to depend on yourself, and perhaps others admire you as a confident and self-determined woman. Eventually, however, you will reach the limits of your understanding, and that's where you will find either frustration—or God. Use fully the gifts of intellect and ability He has given you, but at the same time, put your heart's trust in God. He alone knows no limits.

> Those who know the LORD trust him, because he
> will not leave those who come to him.
>
> PSALM 9:10 NCV

*Y*ou've learned. You're more cautious than you used to be about putting your trust in anyone or in any thing. But remember where you had put your broken trust—in the faithfulness of a person; in the loyalty of your employer; in the strength of the economy. All these earthly things can fail you. React not by withholding trust but by putting your ultimate trust in God. Then all other aspects of trust will, in turn, fall into the right places.

Wisdom

Wisdom is a tree of life to those who embrace her;
happy are those who hold her tightly.

PROVERBS 3:18 NLT

$\mathcal{P}$erhaps you thought you had a great idea, but it turned out to be a big mistake. You wish you had listened to warnings and given the matter more thought. Let God use this teachable moment to give you the gift of wisdom. The wisdom from above may seem counterintuitive at times, but you can be certain it won't fail you. It is embedded in the timeless nature of God, who sees from eternity to eternity.

_____

_____

_____

_____

_____

_____

_____

_____

_____

> If any of you needs wisdom, you should ask God for it.
> He is generous to everyone and will give you wisdom
> without criticizing you.
>
> JAMES 1:5 NCV

$\mathcal{W}$isdom seems like such a lofty goal, yet it's what God offers to you freely and generously simply for the asking. You see, His wisdom has nothing to do with graduate degrees but everything to do with a humble willingness to sit in the school of the Holy Spirit. Open His Word and learn from it. Meditate on its meaning and apply it to your heart and your life. This is genuine wisdom.

Work

"Do not work for food that spoils, but for food that endures to eternal life, which the Son of Man will give you. On him God the Father has placed his seal of approval."

JOHN 6:27

All of us must work for the food that sustains our lives here on earth. But God would remind us that we should work for our spiritual food as well. The Bible says that Jesus is the Bread of Life. Your relationship with Him provides you with food for your spirit, food like wisdom, understanding, insight, and counsel—food like joy, peace, love, and patience. Work hard to provide your spirit with all the spiritual food it needs.

_____

_____

_____

_____

_____

_____

_____

_____

_____

_____

> Serve wholeheartedly, as if you were serving the Lord, not men,
> because you know that the Lord will reward everyone for whatever
> good he does, whether he is slave or free.
>
> EPHESIANS 6:7-8

Sometimes you may find your work unsatisfying, perhaps because you feel unappreciated or unenthusiastic about your daily responsibilities. While praying about any changes you might want to make, remind yourself of the reality of all godly work: God is the boss. Talk to Him about your work in light of the fact that, in all you do, you are doing it for Him. There's great comfort in seeing all you do as your gift to Him.

Worry

[Jesus said]: "Don't worry. . . .Your heavenly Father
already knows all your needs."

MATTHEW 6:31–32 NLT

*W*orry will steal your life if you let it. And yet it is nothing more than the anticipation of trouble that most likely will never come your way. It has no substance and no power except in your mind. God asks you to replace your worry with a firm trust in His love and concern for you. He knows all that is in your future, all of your needs, and He is committed to caring for you. Surrender your mind to God and don't give worry a second thought.

....

....

....

....

....

....

....

....

....

[Jesus said,] "Give your entire attention to what
God is doing right now, and don't get worked up
about what may or may not happen tomorrow."

MATTHEW 6:34 MSG

God considers worry a negative commodity in your life because it takes the
place of trust in His willingness and ability to take care of you. When worry
visits your heart, banish it by reminding yourself how completely God has
taken care of you in the past. List the blessings in your life today that shout
of His protection and love. Then entrust the future to this same God. See for
yourself you have nothing to worry about.

Scripture Index

Old Testament

Psalms

Proverbs

Jeremiah

Hosea

Micah

New Testament

Matthew

Mark

Luke

John

1 Peter

1 John

Topical Index